Influx

John Shenton

Published by John Shenton, 2024.

INFLUX

First edition. September 24, 2024.

ISBN: 979-8227556509

Written by John Shenton.

Also by John Shenton

Table of Contents

Foreward

This book comprehensively explores one of the most pressing global issues today: mass migration. With migration influencing political, economic, and cultural dynamics across continents, the book delves into the root causes, impacts, and underlying forces behind the large-scale movement of people, particularly towards Western nations.

The journey begins with an analysis of the root causes of mass migration, examining the roles of conflict, economic instability, and environmental pressures (Chapter 1). It then questions why neighbouring Arab nations have been reluctant to offer significant support to Middle Eastern migrants (Chapter 2), despite geographic proximity and cultural ties.

Chapter 3 takes a critical look at the toll of third-world emigration on public resources in host countries, questioning whether the benefits of immigration justify the strain on services like healthcare, education, and housing. The focus shifts to closed-border policies in nations like China, Russia, Iran, and North Korea in Chapter 4, examining their strict immigration stances and the ideologies behind them.

From a Western political perspective, Chapter 5 explores how some factions may benefit from mass illegal migration, analyzing whether these movements provide political leverage. Chapter 6 follows the money trail, uncovering the financial drivers behind illegal migration and who stands to profit.

Chapter 7 turns to the cultural impact of mass migration, looking at how the identity of host nations is transformed by the influx of new populations. In Chapter 8, the provocative concept of hybrid warfare is introduced, asking whether mass migration could be weaponized by hostile actors to destabilize nations.

The promoters behind mass migration to the West are scrutinised in Chapter 9, uncovering the political, ideological, and economic forces driving the phenomenon. The financial burden on public systems is further examined in Chapter 10, questioning the long-term sustainability of this influx for Western nations.

Chapter 11 takes on the challenge of governance, probing whether law enforcement and border control agencies are compromised or ill-equipped to manage the scale of illegal migration. Finally, Chapter 12 offers practical solutions for the US, UK, and Europe to address the challenges of mass migration, emphasizing a multi-faceted approach that includes stricter enforcement, international cooperation, and addressing root causes.

This book provides a thought-provoking and nuanced discussion of mass migration, blending geopolitical analysis, economic investigation, and cultural insights to provide a well-rounded understanding of this complex global issue.

Chapter 1: The Root Causes of Mass Migration

Mass migration has become one of the defining issues of the modern world, as millions of people leave their homes, often undertaking dangerous and arduous journeys to seek better lives in distant countries. While migration is driven by multiple factors political, economic, social, and environmental the scale of today's migration, particularly illegal migration, is shaped by a confluence of failures within home countries and the policies of destination countries. Political instability, economic disparity, organised crime, environmental degradation, extremism, and global inequality have created unbearable conditions for many. At the same time, open-door immigration policies in countries like the United States, Canada, the UK, and across Western Europe have served as magnets for mass migration, particularly illegal migration. This chapter delves into the root causes of migration and explores how domestic instability in regions such as Latin America, Africa, and the Middle East intersects with the policies of wealthier nations, contributing to the phenomenon.

1.1 Political Instability, Extremism, and the Role of Iran

One of the foremost drivers of migration from the Middle East is political instability, often exacerbated by extremism and foreign interference. In this region, groups funded and supported by Iran have played a destabilizing role, pushing countries into prolonged conflict and forcing millions of people to flee their homes. Iran has used proxy militias to expand its influence, particularly in Lebanon, Syria, Iraq, and Yemen. These Iranian-backed groups, such as Hezbollah, have perpetuated cycles of violence that make everyday life untenable for civilians, leaving them with little choice but to seek safety elsewhere.

The Syrian Civil War, which has raged for over a decade, offers a clear example of how Iran's support for the Assad regime and its allied militias has contributed to a humanitarian disaster. Millions of Syrians have been displaced by bombings, chemical attacks, and other atrocities, and many have made perilous journeys to Europe. Similarly, in Yemen, the Iran-backed Houthi rebels have prolonged a devastating war, contributing to a famine and the collapse of basic services, further exacerbating the refugee crisis in the region.

The U.S. withdrawal from Afghanistan in 2021, under the Biden-Harris administration, further destabilized Central Asia. The abrupt nature of the withdrawal left Afghanistan vulnerable to the rapid takeover by the Taliban, plunging the country back into an authoritarian regime marked by violence, persecution, and economic collapse. Many Afghans who had worked with Western forces or hoped for a more open society were left stranded and vulnerable, resulting in a new wave of migration as people sought refuge from the Taliban's rule.

1.2 Socialist Ideology, Drug Cartels, and Organized Crime

Latin America, particularly in countries like Venezuela, Nicaragua, and Cuba, has been severely impacted by socialist regimes whose policies, in theory, promise equality and prosperity but in practice have resulted in corruption, poverty, and the erosion of civil liberties. Venezuela, once a wealthy nation, has been plunged into economic ruin under the leadership of Nicolás Maduro. The government's authoritarian grip, alongside economic mismanagement, has led to hyperinflation, shortages of basic goods, and a healthcare system in collapse. Millions of Venezuelans have fled to neighbouring countries and beyond in search of food, employment, and medical care.

In Central America, socialist-leaning

governments, often intertwined with drug cartels, have fostered environments of lawlessness and violence. Honduras, Guatemala, and El Salvador, collectively known as the Northern Triangle, suffer from a toxic combination of corrupt governance, organized crime, and extreme poverty. Drug cartels, gangs, and criminal organizations have infiltrated these countries, creating conditions so dangerous that citizens have little hope of building stable lives. Consequently, many are driven north toward the United States. However, a significant proportion of these migrants are economic migrants, seeking better living conditions and opportunities rather than fleeing direct persecution.

While violence is a key push factor, the socialist ideologies in these regions have also failed to create sustainable economies, pushing more and more people into economic migration. Organized crime, particularly drug cartels, exploits the political and economic instability, profiting from human trafficking, smuggling operations, and violence that further drives people out of their home countries.

1.3 Economic Disparity and Migration by Choice

While many migrants are fleeing war and violence, a growing number are economic migrants people who choose to leave their countries primarily for financial reasons, hoping to find better opportunities in wealthier nations. Recently, there has been a notable increase in Chinese migrants heading to the United States and Western countries. These individuals are not fleeing political persecution or environmental disaster but are driven by a desire for better economic opportunities and personal freedoms that are harder to find within China's increasingly controlled economy and political system. These migrants highlight an important aspect of contemporary migration while some people are forced to leave due to dire circumstances, others make the conscious decision to move in search of a better life, adding further strain to already overburdened immigration systems.

In regions like Latin America, many economic migrants see the wealth and opportunity of the United States, Canada, and Europe as their best chance for upward mobility. The poverty in countries like Haiti, where economic conditions have stagnated for decades, drives thousands of people to risk dangerous journeys, often with the assistance of smuggling networks, to enter countries with more favourable job markets.

1.4 Climate Change and Environmental Displacement

Another increasingly prominent factor in mass migration is climate change. Regions in sub-Saharan Africa, Latin America, and Southeast Asia are being hit hard by environmental degradation, such as desertification, droughts, and rising sea levels. These environmental shifts are especially devastating in poorer countries, where agriculture is often the primary livelihood. As crops fail and water sources dry up, millions of people are forced to leave their homes in search of more hospitable areas.

The Sahel region of Africa, which spans countries like Mali, Niger, and Chad, has experienced severe desertification. Farmers and herders in this region are unable to sustain their livelihoods, prompting widespread migration, both within Africa and toward Europe. Climate-induced migration is likely to increase in the coming decades, further exacerbating global migration trends.

1.5 Open-Door Policies and Western Foreign Policy's Role

Open-door immigration policies in Western nations have unintentionally acted as a magnet for illegal migration. Countries like the United States, Canada, the UK, and many in Western Europe have historically maintained relatively generous immigration and asylum policies, particularly in response to humanitarian crises. These policies, while well-intentioned, have also had the unintended consequence of encouraging greater numbers of illegal migrants, many of whom are not fleeing persecution but are seeking better economic opportunities. This surge is compounded by messaging from political figures that suggest a welcome reception for migrants, leading people to believe that once they reach the borders of these nations, they will be allowed to stay.

In the United States, under the Biden-Harris administration, changes in immigration enforcement, particularly at the southern border, have been interpreted by many as signalling more lenient policies. This perception, whether accurate or not, has fueled a significant rise in illegal border crossings. Migrants from across Latin America, and even from distant regions like Africa and China, have attempted to enter the U.S., drawn by the belief that the risk is worth the potential reward.

Europe, too, has seen waves of migrants drawn by its more liberal asylum policies. Germany, for instance, has faced immense pressure since opening its doors to refugees during the Syrian Civil War, and other countries like the UK and France have seen increased illegal immigration due to a perceived path toward citizenship or asylum. While these policies reflect the humanitarian values of these nations, they also attract economic migrants who see an opportunity to bypass legal immigration routes.

Global inequality and Western foreign policy have also played a role in exacerbating migration trends. U.S. interventions in the Middle East, such as the 2003 invasion of Iraq and the more recent withdrawal from Afghanistan, have destabilized entire regions, contributing to large-scale displacement. Similarly, U.S. policies in Latin America, particularly during the Cold War, supported authoritarian regimes and contributed to long-term instability, creating environments that now drive migration toward the U.S. and Canada.

Conclusion

Mass migration is a complex and multifaceted phenomenon, driven by a variety of forces ranging from political instability, extremism, and organized crime to economic disparity, climate change, and open-door immigration policies in wealthier nations. While many migrants are forced to leave their homes due to war, persecution, or environmental disasters, a significant number are economic migrants who seek better opportunities in Western countries. The open-door policies of the U.S., Canada, the UK, and Western Europe, though grounded in humanitarian ideals, have become magnets for illegal migration, contributing to both domestic tensions and the global migration crisis.

To effectively address the issue of mass migration, policymakers must tackle the root causes in migrants' home countries whether it be failed governance, extremist movements, socialist regimes entangled with organized crime, or economic and environmental collapse while also rethinking the long-term impacts of their immigration policies. Without a comprehensive and balanced approach that addresses both the push and pull factors driving migration, the pressures on both origin and destination countries will continue to grow.

Chapter 2: Why Aren't Neighboring Arab Countries Supporting Middle Eastern Migrants?

In the preceding chapter, we explored mass migration as a global phenomenon, driven by factors such as conflict, environmental degradation, economic disparity, and political instability. The Middle East, a region long plagued by war and unrest, has been one of the most significant sources of refugee flows in recent decades. As civil wars, insurgencies, and authoritarian regimes have displaced millions of people, many would expect neighbouring Arab countries to take a leading role in offering sanctuary to those fleeing persecution. Given the shared cultural, religious, and linguistic ties that bind many Middle Eastern nations together, this expectation seems natural. Yet, in reality, the opposite has often been true. The reluctance of Arab states to fully embrace refugees from nations such as Syria, Yemen, and Iraq raises complex questions about regional politics, security concerns, and domestic priorities.

This chapter delves into why some Arab countries, despite their proximity and common heritage, have taken a limited or cautious approach to accommodating their fellow Middle Eastern migrants. A close examination of geopolitical interests, national security fears, economic factors, and internal political dynamics reveals a more intricate narrative that challenges any simplistic notion of solidarity within the Arab world.

Historical and Geopolitical Context

To understand the current stance of many Arab nations toward refugees, it is essential to place it within the broader historical and geopolitical framework of the region. The Middle East has long been a cauldron of external interference, colonial legacies, and artificial borders drawn without regard for ethnic or tribal allegiances. These imposed divisions have often led to fragile statehood, internal conflicts, and tensions between neighbouring countries.

The Arab states that formed after the dissolution of the Ottoman Empire in the early 20th century were forged in the fires of anti-colonialism, tribal rivalry, and nationalist movements. In many cases, ruling regimes have remained wary of external influences, seeing the presence of foreign populations whether migrants, refugees, or expatriates as a potential threat to their national identity and stability. Moreover, power dynamics between Arab states themselves have often been marked by rivalry and distrust, particularly along sectarian lines, as seen between Sunni-majority countries like Saudi Arabia and Shia-majority Iran. In this context, opening the borders to waves of migrants can be perceived not merely as a humanitarian challenge but as a risk to the internal coherence of already delicate political systems.

National Security Concerns

One of the foremost reasons Arab states have been reluctant to accept large numbers of migrants is the potential threat to national security. Many countries in the region are themselves deeply fragile, with governance structures that struggle to maintain control over their populations. For example, Jordan and Lebanon, which have hosted large numbers of Palestinian refugees since the mid-20th century, have faced enormous challenges in maintaining security and social cohesion. The fear of importing conflicts and exacerbating sectarian divisions is very real.

Syria's civil war, for instance, has not only displaced millions of people but has also fueled the rise of extremist groups such as ISIS. Neighbouring states like Jordan, Lebanon, and Turkey have experienced the destabilizing effects of refugees fleeing the Syrian conflict, and other Arab nations, particularly in the Gulf, are wary of allowing similar scenarios to unfold within their borders. Countries like Saudi Arabia, Kuwait, and the United Arab Emirates have large expatriate populations that already present challenges in terms of integration and national identity, and these states may fear that taking in refugees could increase the risk of radicalization, internal dissent, or even terrorism.

In addition, some Arab governments are concerned that accepting refugees would involve an implicit political statement about the causes of these conflicts. For example, Saudi Arabia and its allies have been deeply involved in the Yemeni civil war, supporting the internationally recognized government against the Iranian-backed Houthi rebels. For these countries, accepting large numbers of Yemeni refugees could be seen as a tacit acknowledgement of their failure to bring about stability in Yemen or as a gesture that undermines their military objectives. In the case of Iraq, the sectarian nature of its conflict with a Sunni minority that felt marginalized under the Shia-dominated government poses similar risks for neighbouring Arab states that fear importing sectarian divisions and conflict.

Economic Strain and Resource Limitations

While wealthy Gulf states like Saudi Arabia, the

UAE, and Qatar are often accused of shirking their responsibilities in providing asylum, it is essential to recognize the economic calculations that underpin their decisions. Although these countries are financially prosperous, their economies rely heavily on foreign labour, particularly in the construction, oil, and service sectors. This reliance on migrant workers from South Asia and other regions creates a delicate economic balance that could be disrupted by the influx of refugees. These workers, typically part of a structured labour system, are employed on specific terms with little room for integration into society. In contrast, refugees arriving from conflict zones often bring with them a host of challenges, from the need for housing and healthcare to the long-term demands of education and employment.

The Gulf countries also face significant concerns about the sustainability of their welfare systems and public services. Accepting large numbers of refugees could place an unsustainable burden on healthcare, education, and infrastructure, particularly in countries where native populations already benefit from generous state subsidies and services. The risk of diluting these benefits and creating public dissatisfaction may further deter these nations from offering refuge.

Similarly, even countries like Jordan and Lebanon, which have been lauded for accepting large numbers of Syrian refugees, have struggled to meet the economic demands created by their humanitarian efforts. Jordan, in particular, faces water shortages, high unemployment, and limited fiscal capacity, all of which have been exacerbated by the presence of over a million Syrian refugees. The international community has provided some financial support, but it has often been insufficient to cover the full costs. As a result, host countries have sometimes had to impose restrictions on refugee employment, housing, and movement, creating tensions both within their societies and among the refugee populations.

Demographic and Political Concerns

Beyond economic and security considerations, many Arab states are also reluctant to accept large numbers of refugees due to concerns about the potential for demographic and political change. Countries in the Gulf Cooperation Council (GCC), for example, have small native populations in comparison to the vast numbers of expatriates and foreign workers residing within their borders. Introducing significant numbers of refugees could further dilute the demographic composition of these countries, raising questions about national identity, citizenship, and political representation.

The issue of demographics is particularly sensitive in countries that are already balancing ethnic or sectarian tensions. Lebanon, with its fragile sectarian political system, has long struggled to maintain peace between its Christian, Sunni, and Shia communities. The arrival of over a million Syrian refugees, many of whom are Sunni Muslims, has significantly altered the country's demographic balance, creating fears among some Lebanese groups that their political influence could be diminished. The potential for similar concerns in other Arab states, particularly those with significant minority populations, cannot be overlooked.

Furthermore, some regimes fear that accepting large numbers of refugees could inspire political unrest or embolden opposition movements. Refugee populations, particularly those fleeing authoritarian rule, may bring with them demands for political rights, freedom of expression, and democratic governance ideas that could be seen as threatening by the often autocratic regimes of the Middle East. The Arab Spring, which began in 2011 as a wave of pro-democracy protests, remains a potent reminder for many of the potential for mass movements to destabilize even the most entrenched rulers.

Conclusion: A Complex Calculus of Refugee Politics

The reluctance of many Arab states to accept migrants from neighbouring countries is the result of a complex interplay of geopolitical, economic, and social factors. National security concerns, economic limitations, and demographic anxieties all play a role in shaping the policies of countries across the Middle East, from the oil-rich Gulf states to the economically struggling nations of Jordan and Lebanon. While cultural and religious commonalities might suggest a natural solidarity, the political realities of the region have led many governments to adopt more cautious or restrictive approaches to migration.

In the broader context of global migration, the case of the Middle East illustrates the limits of humanitarianism in the face of national self-interest. As millions of refugees continue to seek safety and stability, the challenges of accommodating them will remain a significant issue, not only for the Arab world but for the international community as a whole. Understanding the reluctance of neighbouring Arab states is essential in addressing the broader question of how to manage migration in a region where political instability, economic fragility, and internal divisions often take precedence over humanitarian concerns. The path forward requires not only more robust international cooperation but also a deeper engagement with the regional realities that continue to shape migration policies.

Chapter 3: Third-World Emigration: A Drain on Public Resources?

The global migration crisis is one of the most pressing issues facing the Western world today. Over the past several decades, waves of migrants, particularly from developing or war-torn nations, have moved to more affluent Western countries, seeking better lives. While immigration has historically been a cornerstone for cultural and economic growth, especially in countries like the United States and the United Kingdom, the dynamics of large-scale, often uncontrolled immigration have evolved. Today, the conversation is increasingly focused on the strain placed upon public resources healthcare, education, housing, and welfare by waves of migrants, many of whom arrive without significant financial resources, language proficiency, or immediately marketable skills.

This chapter will explore how illegal or unregulated immigration, particularly from third-world nations, is impacting the social fabric and public resources of nations like the United States, the United Kingdom, Canada, and Western Europe. We will also examine how policymakers and bureaucracies, particularly in Brussels for the EU and the Biden-Harris administration in the United States, have responded or failed to respond to these challenges, and whether their policies reflect a lack of empathy for their citizens.

1. Financial Strain on Public Resources

Healthcare Systems Under Pressure

One of the most immediate impacts of large-scale immigration is on national healthcare systems. In the United States, the UK, Canada, and Western Europe, healthcare is often considered a public good, either through fully or partially subsidized healthcare systems. However, the influx of migrants who may not have legal status, health insurance, or the ability to contribute to the healthcare system often places an outsized burden on these systems.

- **United States:** In the US, many undocumented migrants use emergency services, which cannot legally turn anyone away. Hospitals, particularly those near the southern border, face overcrowded emergency rooms and increased costs to treat uninsured, undocumented migrants. The Biden-Harris administration's lax border enforcement has exacerbated this issue. Some states, such as Texas and Arizona, bear the brunt of these costs, straining their healthcare budgets and forcing hospitals to either cut back on services or pass costs to taxpayers and insured patients.

- **United Kingdom:** The UK's National Health Service (NHS), long regarded as one of the most robust public healthcare systems in the world, has also been stretched to its limits by the surge in immigration. The system has seen increased pressure on general practitioners (GPs), hospital services, and mental health resources as migrants, many of whom lack adequate health records or speak little English, require care. Critics argue that while the NHS was designed to serve the British population, it is now burdened with providing healthcare to a much larger, non-contributing migrant population.

- **Canada:** Canada's universal healthcare system also faces similar challenges. Migrants, particularly asylum seekers and those entering through unofficial crossings, contribute to a growing backlog in medical appointments and services. This is particularly acute in major cities like Toronto and Montreal, where hospitals are overburdened, and citizens often face longer waiting times for services.

- **Western Europe:** In countries like Germany, France, and Sweden, the strain on healthcare is profound. After welcoming millions of migrants, particularly from Syria, Afghanistan, and Africa, these countries are grappling with the financial burden of providing medical care to newcomers, many of whom arrive with untreated chronic conditions or need long-term care. In Sweden, for example, emergency services have been overwhelmed, and there is a noticeable shortage of healthcare professionals capable of treating both the native and migrant populations effectively. Critics in these nations have begun to question whether the state can maintain its generous healthcare systems while absorbing so many newcomers.

Education: Struggling to Integrate

Another major area where immigration places strain is education. Public school systems in many Western nations are grappling with the arrival of children who often do not speak the local language, have limited formal education, or come from traumatic backgrounds. The costs of educating these children often fall on already overstretched school systems.

- **United States:** In the US, schools near the southern border and in major cities are struggling with an influx of non-English-speaking students, many of whom require specialized teachers and resources. These resources, including English as a Second Language (ESL) programs, come at the expense of other educational priorities. Additionally, the social integration of these children can be challenging, and schools with large migrant populations often suffer from reduced academic outcomes, negatively affecting native-born students.

- **United Kingdom:** Schools in the UK face similar challenges. Many urban schools now have a majority of students for whom English is a second language, requiring significant investment in language and support services. This also often slows down the overall pace of instruction, leading to frustrations among both teachers and parents of British-born children. The burden on schools to provide services like translation and special education for trauma-affected students has created an uneven educational experience.
- **Canada:** Canada, with its officially bilingual status, already spends significant resources on accommodating linguistic diversity. However, the influx of third-world immigrants, particularly in urban centres, has added a layer of complexity. Schools must navigate the needs of students speaking dozens of different languages while maintaining academic standards for all. The result is often diluted educational quality and increasing frustration among native-born Canadians.
- **Western Europe:** Countries like Germany and France, which have accepted large numbers of refugees and migrants, face significant challenges in integrating these students into their education systems. Many schools are overpopulated, teachers are overworked, and resources are stretched thin. In France, for example, schools in immigrant-heavy areas have seen a decline in academic performance as teachers struggle to accommodate large numbers of non-French-speaking students. Germany has invested heavily in integration programs, but the cost of such programs has been a point of political contention.

Housing: A Growing Crisis

The demand for affordable housing has increased dramatically in countries facing large-scale immigration, exacerbating housing crises that already existed in major cities.

- **United States:** In cities like New York, Los Angeles, and Miami, housing shortages are common, and the influx of migrants has worsened the situation. Illegal immigrants often occupy low-income housing or overcrowded apartments, driving up rental prices for native-born citizens and creating competition for limited affordable housing units. Programs designed to assist low-income citizens now also cater to migrant families, creating longer waiting lists and further frustrating American citizens.
- **United Kingdom:** The housing crisis in the UK is well-documented, with affordable housing in short supply. Migrants, particularly those seeking asylum, are often housed in government-funded accommodations. However, the influx has put immense pressure on local councils to provide housing, leading to skyrocketing rental prices and longer waiting lists for social housing. The result is an ongoing debate about whether native-born Britons are being unfairly displaced by newcomers.
- **Canada:** The housing crisis in Canadian cities like Toronto and Vancouver has also worsened due to immigration. Migrants, many of whom lack the financial means to secure housing independently, are often placed in government-subsidized housing. This has driven up rental prices and reduced the availability of affordable housing for Canadian citizens, creating political tension and resentment.
- **Western Europe:** Western Europe, particularly countries like Germany, France, and Sweden, faces a similar problem. The

sheer number of migrants has overwhelmed housing services, forcing some governments to convert sports arenas, schools, and hotels into temporary shelters. Long-term housing solutions are expensive and difficult to implement, leaving many native-born citizens frustrated as they compete for limited resources.

2. Economic Impact: Labor Markets and Wage Suppression
Large-scale migration also has a significant impact on labour markets, particularly in industries that rely on unskilled or semi-skilled labour.

- **United States:** In the US, the influx of undocumented immigrants, many of whom take low-wage jobs, has led to wage suppression in industries such as agriculture, construction, and hospitality. While businesses benefit from a cheap labour force, native-born workers often find themselves competing for jobs at lower wages. This has created a divide between political elites and working-class Americans, particularly those who feel that their economic prospects have been undermined by lax immigration policies.
- **United Kingdom:** Brexit was, in many ways, a referendum on immigration. Many British citizens, particularly those in the working class, felt that the free movement of labour from within the EU and beyond was driving down wages and reducing job opportunities for British-born workers. While post-Brexit immigration policies have sought to address these concerns, the arrival of migrants from third-world countries continues to place pressure on the labour market, particularly in low-wage sectors.
- **Canada:** Canada's labour market, particularly in major cities, has also seen downward pressure on wages in industries that

rely on migrant labour. While Canada's immigration system is points-based, prioritizing skilled workers, the influx of refugees and asylum seekers has created competition in lower-wage sectors, frustrating native-born workers.

- **Western Europe:** In Western Europe, countries like Germany and Sweden have seen similar effects. While migrants fill low-wage jobs, particularly in the service and agricultural sectors, they also create competition for native workers, leading to wage suppression. This has fueled anti-immigrant sentiment and increased support for far-right political parties in many of these nations.

3. Government Response: A Lack of Empathy for Citizens?

Despite the mounting evidence of the strain that immigration places on public resources, many Western governments have shown little sympathy for their citizens who bear the brunt of these changes.

- **United States:** The Biden-Harris administration has faced criticism for its handling of immigration, particularly at the southern border. Critics argue that the administration's policies are driven more by ideological commitments to open borders than by a genuine concern for the well-being of American citizens. Border enforcement has been lax, and while the administration has provided services to migrants, many American citizens feel neglected as their communities face increased competition for jobs, housing, and healthcare.
- **United Kingdom:** In the UK, the post-Brexit Conservative government has promised to "take back control" of immigration. However, many Britons feel that the government's focus has been on appeasing Brussels and international organizations rather than addressing the concerns of British citizens. The housing and healthcare crises

continue to escalate, and many believe that the government's priorities are misplaced.

- **Canada:** The Canadian government, under Prime Minister Justin Trudeau, has taken a welcoming approach to immigration, particularly for refugees and asylum seekers. However, this has led to criticism that the government is more concerned with maintaining its international image than with addressing the concerns of Canadian citizens. Housing shortages, healthcare backlogs, and wage suppression are growing problems, yet the government seems unwilling to restrict immigration in any meaningful way.

- **Western Europe:** In Western Europe, the bureaucrats in Brussels who govern the European Union have been particularly unsympathetic to the concerns of EU citizens. The EU's commitment to open borders and the free movement of labour, combined with its relatively lax asylum policies, has led to growing frustration among the citizens of member states. Countries like Italy, Greece, and Hungary have pushed back against the EU's immigration policies, arguing that their own citizens' needs are being ignored in favour of accommodating migrants.

Conclusion

Large-scale migration from third-world countries presents profound challenges to Western nations. The strain on public resources healthcare, education, housing, and welfare cannot be ignored. While migration can bring cultural and economic benefits, the unregulated or poorly managed influx of migrants without skills, language proficiency, or financial resources places a heavy burden on the host nations. Governments must balance their humanitarian obligations with the needs of their citizens, and yet, as we have seen, many seem more focused on appeasing international organizations or pursuing ideological goals. The result is growing dissatisfaction among native-born citizens, who feel that their governments are failing to prioritize their welfare.

Chapter 4: Closed Borders: China, Russia, Iran, and North Korea's Stance on Immigration

In the 21st century, mass migration has become a central issue for many Western democracies. Faced with both economic opportunities and humanitarian crises, these nations have often struggled with the balance between open borders and the challenges of integrating large numbers of immigrants. Previous chapters explored how mass migration toward Western nations has been fueled by conflict, poverty, and the dream of better opportunities, often juxtaposed against the reluctance of wealthy Arab nations to absorb refugees, despite their geographical proximity and shared cultural ties. Iran, in particular, has been a source of tension and instability in the Middle East, exacerbating many of the regional conflicts that have contributed to the refugee crisis. Meanwhile, Russia's invasion of Ukraine and the broader strategic implications of China's increasingly assertive global posture have raised concerns about their role in shaping the global order, including through hybrid warfare tactics. However, one notable distinction between these authoritarian regimes and the West is their strict control over both immigration and emigration.

This chapter focuses on the closed-border policies of four key authoritarian regimes: China, Russia, Iran, and North Korea. These nations exhibit varying degrees of restriction on the movement of people, but all share a commonality in using immigration controls as a tool of social control, national security, and economic management. Understanding their approaches provides insight into how geopolitical strategies, domestic policies, and ideological underpinnings shape global migration trends, presenting a stark contrast to the policies of Western democracies.

China: Economic Growth and Social Stability Through Control

China's stance on immigration is heavily shaped by its authoritarian governance and long-standing emphasis on maintaining social harmony. Immigration, whether into or out of the country, is seen as a factor that could upset the delicate balance of power between the Communist Party and the population. This has led to tight control over who is allowed to enter and leave the country, with a focus on preserving national security and social stability.

Internal Migration and the Hukou System

China has long had an internal migration system that prioritizes control. The "hukou" system, a household registration mechanism, ties people to their place of birth and limits their access to social services in other regions. This has allowed the Chinese government to control the flow of workers, ensuring that economic hubs like Beijing and Shanghai do not become overwhelmed by rural migrants seeking better opportunities. While this system has loosened over the years to accommodate the needs of China's rapidly growing economy, it remains an essential tool of social control.

Limited Immigration Policies

Immigration into China is also highly restricted. Foreign workers are generally welcomed only in specialized fields that align with the government's economic priorities, such as technology, engineering, and scientific research. Unlike Western democracies, China does not see immigration to boost its workforce or population growth. Instead, it focuses on domestic population management, utilizing tools such as the One-Child Policy (now modified to encourage more births) to influence demographic trends.

Geopolitical Impact: Belt and Road and Hybrid Warfare

China's global stance also plays into its immigration policies. While it engages in massive infrastructure projects through its Belt and Road Initiative (BRI), fostering economic ties with many developing nations, it does not encourage mass migration into China from these regions. However, China's hybrid warfare strategy utilizing economic influence, cyber operations, and propaganda suggests that immigration policies are but one facet of its broader geopolitical aims. Through hybrid warfare tactics, China seeks to influence other nations while maintaining internal cohesion, leveraging its global influence without opening its borders.

Russia: Nationalism, Security, and Demographic Control

Russia, under the leadership of Vladimir Putin, has pursued an increasingly nationalist and militaristic path. Immigration policy in Russia is tied to its broader goal of preserving national unity and mitigating what the Kremlin views as external threats. Russia's strict control over immigration is not only a domestic concern but also a reflection of its aggressive foreign policy, particularly in the context of its military invasion of Ukraine.

Population Management and Economic Challenges

Russia faces significant demographic challenges, including a declining population and a shrinking labour force. In theory, immigration could help offset these trends. However, the Russian government remains hesitant to open its borders, partly due to concerns over the integration of non-Russian ethnic groups and the potential for social unrest. Instead, Russia relies on its vast internal resources and authoritarian controls to maintain its workforce.

Security Concerns and Ethnic Nationalism

Russia's historical fear of external threats whether from the West or its southern neighbours in Central Asia has deeply influenced its immigration policies. There is a strong emphasis on maintaining ethnic homogeneity, and immigration from regions outside of the former Soviet Union is tightly controlled. The rise of nationalist rhetoric has further amplified these concerns, with Putin positioning himself as the defender of Russian cultural identity. This has led to restrictive immigration policies, even as Russia seeks to project power abroad.

Hybrid Warfare and Strategic Displacement

Like China, Russia employs hybrid warfare tactics to influence global affairs. In the context of migration, Russia's involvement in Syria and other conflict zones has exacerbated refugee crises, indirectly increasing migration flows toward Europe. Russia benefits from the destabilization of its geopolitical rivals while maintaining strict controls over its borders. This tactic of displacement has become a key feature of Russia's foreign policy, allowing it to manipulate migration trends without suffering the domestic consequences of large-scale immigration.

Iran: Theocratic Control and Sectarian Politics

Iran's immigration policy is deeply intertwined with its theocratic governance and regional ambitions. While Iran is home to a large number of refugees, primarily from Afghanistan, it tightly controls who is allowed to settle within its borders and under what conditions. This reflects both the regime's desire for social control and its broader geopolitical strategy in the Middle East.

Refugees and Sectarianism

Iran has a long history of hosting refugees, particularly from war-torn Afghanistan and Iraq. However, these populations are often marginalized and live under strict conditions. Iran's primary concern is maintaining its Shia theocratic identity, and immigration policies are shaped by this goal. Refugees who do not fit within Iran's sectarian framework are often treated as second-class citizens if not outright denied entry.

Regional Influence and Proxy Conflicts

Iran's involvement in conflicts across the Middle East most notably in Syria, Iraq, and Yemen has contributed to mass displacement and migration. Like Russia, Iran benefits from destabilizing its rivals while maintaining internal control over its population. The regime uses proxy groups and militias to assert its influence in the region, further complicating migration patterns as people flee conflict zones. Despite its involvement in these conflicts, Iran remains reluctant to allow large numbers of refugees to permanently settle within its borders, preferring instead to use migration as a tool of leverage in its geopolitical strategy.

North Korea: Isolationism as Policy

North Korea represents perhaps the most extreme example of closed borders. The regime's isolationist policies under Kim Jong-un are designed to prevent both immigration and emigration, with the state exercising complete control over the movement of its citizens. The reasons for this are primarily rooted in maintaining the regime's absolute control over the population and preventing the influx of external influences.

Totalitarian Control Over Movement

North Korea's regime views migration as a threat to its survival. Citizens are prohibited from leaving the country without state permission, and those who attempt to flee often face severe punishment. Likewise, the regime does not encourage foreign immigration, seeing outsiders as potential sources of dissent and disruption. This isolationist stance is a hallmark of North Korea's approach to governance, where maintaining control over the population is prioritized above all else.

Geopolitical Isolation and Propaganda

North Korea's closed-border policies are closely tied to its broader geopolitical isolation. The regime uses propaganda to promote the idea that North Korea is superior to the outside world, justifying its strict control over movement as necessary for national security. While the regime occasionally engages with the international community, particularly in negotiations over its nuclear program, it remains deeply suspicious of any outside influence. This isolationism extends to its immigration policies, ensuring that the regime remains insulated from external pressures.

Conclusion: Closed Borders and Global Implications

The closed-border policies of China, Russia, Iran, and North Korea stand in stark contrast to the more open approaches of many Western democracies. These authoritarian regimes view immigration not as an opportunity but as a potential threat to their internal stability, national identity, and geopolitical ambitions. While Western nations grapple with the challenges of mass migration, these regimes maintain strict control over their borders, using immigration policy as a tool for social control and strategic advantage.

At the same time, the actions of these nations on the global stage whether through hybrid warfare, proxy conflicts, or economic influence contribute to the very migration crises they seek to avoid domestically. As the world becomes increasingly interconnected, the divide between open and closed borders will continue to shape global migration patterns, with authoritarian regimes maintaining their insular stance even as their actions reverberate far beyond their borders.

Chapter 5: The Political Advantage of Mass Illegal Migration: A Western Perspective

In this chapter, we explore the dynamics and political advantages of mass illegal migration for various actors in Western societies. Focusing on the United States, United Kingdom, and Europe, we will examine how certain political forces use this complex issue to secure electoral advantages, drive specific economic agendas, and reshape social narratives. As migration flows increase, the narrative of multiculturalism, diversity, and human rights has been co-opted by some political actors, while others frame the issue as an existential threat to cultural identity, economic stability, and national security.

Mass illegal migration, while often portrayed as a humanitarian crisis, offers a complex set of benefits to different political and economic actors, including those in power. This chapter will consider how politicians leverage migration for electoral gains, harness labour market advantages, and manage public opinion, all while revealing deeper fractures in the social contract.

The Weaponization of Multiculturalism and Human Rights

In the past few decades, progressive political parties across the U.S., UK, and Europe have effectively weaponized the rhetoric of multiculturalism and human rights, positioning themselves as champions of inclusion and diversity. This narrative is particularly potent in urban and cosmopolitan areas, where progressive values are more deeply entrenched, and where migrant communities are concentrated.

By portraying mass illegal migration as a moral issue one framed in terms of human rights, refugees fleeing persecution, and the enrichment of society through diversity these political actors often succeed in appealing to voters who place a high value on social justice and inclusivity. This framing reduces the discourse to a binary: those who support migration are compassionate and progressive, while those who oppose it are portrayed as xenophobic, bigoted, or backward.

In this context, opposition to migration whether motivated by cultural concerns or economic realities is frequently delegitimized by the progressive left. Far-right or nationalist groups, in particular, are often portrayed as intolerant or driven by racism, when in fact many of these groups consist of ordinary citizens alarmed by the scale of migration and the profound cultural transformations it brings.

Electoral Gains and the Promise of a New Electorate

A key political advantage for left-leaning parties is the potential electoral gains mass illegal migration can bring. In the U.S., this is most apparent. With legal pathways to citizenship often available after several years, illegal migrants and their descendants can become future voters. Democratic-leaning politicians have increasingly sought to secure pathways to regularization and citizenship for undocumented migrants, recognizing that these individuals are more likely to support parties that advocate for migrant rights and inclusivity.

This demographic shift has the potential to significantly alter the electoral landscape, particularly in areas where migrant populations are dense. As migrants and their children become integrated into the voting public, they often align with political parties that support their right to stay, offer protections, and promote progressive social policies. This, in turn, strengthens the base of these parties, offering a clear, long-term political incentive for maintaining or even encouraging lax immigration enforcement.

In Europe, where electoral systems differ, this dynamic is more nuanced. While migrants may not be able to vote immediately, political parties advocating for open borders or progressive migration policies still benefit from the support of younger, more urbanized voters. In countries like Germany, France, and the UK, where multiculturalism is often championed by the left, supporting migration becomes a way of appealing to voters who see themselves as socially liberal and tolerant.

Far-Right Reactions and the Preservation of National Identity

While progressive parties may reap short-term electoral benefits, mass illegal migration has also energized nationalist, populist, and so-called far-right movements across the West. The left frequently labels these groups as reactionary, framing them as fear-driven movements fueled by racism or xenophobia. However, a more nuanced perspective reveals that many of these groups represent citizens who perceive a deliberate subordination of their culture, values, and national identity by elites, politicians, and business interests who stand to gain from the influx of migrant populations.

For these citizens, mass illegal migration is not simply a question of economic impact or resource strain, but a fundamental threat to the integrity of their societies. They witness rapid demographic changes in their neighbourhoods, increased competition for jobs, housing, and social services, and a dilution of cultural traditions. To them, migration threatens the fabric of their nations whether it be the weakening of social cohesion, the erosion of shared cultural values, or the perception that their homeland is becoming unrecognizable.

Populist movements and so-called far-right parties in Europe and the U.S. have gained traction by addressing these concerns, offering a counter-narrative to the progressive discourse on migration. Leaders of these movements articulate the anxieties of working-class and rural voters who feel left behind in a rapidly globalizing world. Unlike the elites in power, who benefit economically from cheap migrant labour and politically from a more diverse electorate, these citizens bear the brunt of social disruptions. Nationalist leaders speak directly to these concerns, arguing that immigration is a tool used by elites to weaken native populations, both culturally and economically.

Migration as a Tool for Political and Economic Power

From the perspective of many nationalist groups, mass illegal migration is seen as a deliberate tactic used by globalist elites to secure their power and influence. For politicians in Western nations, migration provides a steady supply of low-wage workers who help drive down labour costs and boost corporate profits. Industries such as agriculture, construction, and hospitality, which often depend on cheap labour, benefit enormously from the influx of undocumented migrants willing to work for less than native-born citizens.

Politicians aligned with business interests or neoliberal economic policies often support or tacitly allow high levels of illegal migration to persist because it benefits the corporate class. As wages are suppressed and labour costs minimized, these business sectors generate greater profits. This, in turn, strengthens political alliances between pro-migration politicians and their corporate donors, who benefit financially from the exploitation of migrant labour.

From a political standpoint, these dynamics help maintain a system in which elites consolidate power, using both economic leverage and the support of diverse voting blocs to remain in control. For these elites, mass illegal migration represents a means of creating a more pliable electorate one that can be shaped and directed by progressive policies, ensuring the status quo remains intact. By supporting policies that allow for increased migration, they secure the loyalty of both business interests and migrant communities, thereby fortifying their place within the political and economic hierarchy.

Far-Right Groups as Defenders of Cultural Sovereignty

While often dismissed by the mainstream as extremist, far-right groups and nationalist movements can be seen as a reaction to the manipulation of migration by political and economic elites. For these groups, the influx of migrants is not only an economic issue but a deliberate cultural strategy employed by those in power. They view migration as a way to dilute national identity, weaken civic bonds, and replace the existing population with a more easily controlled demographic.

From this perspective, the far-right frames itself as the defender of national sovereignty, cultural heritage, and the rights of native-born citizens. Their opposition to illegal migration is not merely about race or ethnicity, but about protecting their way of life from being eroded by forces that prioritize wealth, power, and political advantage over the wellbeing of the nation. To them, illegal migration represents a transfer of power from the citizenry to a class of elites who exploit the situation for their gain.

The rise of these nationalist movements demonstrates the extent to which many citizens feel alienated by a political establishment that seems disconnected from their concerns. As migration reshapes their communities, these individuals turn to leaders who speak to their fears, frustrations, and sense of displacement. While the mainstream labels these groups as far-right or extremist, for many, they represent a last line of defence against what they perceive as the systematic undermining of their nation and culture.

Conclusion

Mass illegal migration offers substantial political and economic advantages for certain actors in the West, from progressive politicians seeking a new electorate to business interests relying on cheap labour. The narrative of multiculturalism and human rights has been co-opted as a tool to maintain political power and economic stability for elites, often at the expense of native populations who see their cultural and economic position eroded.

However, this political advantage is not without consequences. The rise of far-right and nationalist movements signals a growing discontent among citizens who feel their voices are being drowned out by elites more concerned with wealth, power, and the maintenance of their status. For these groups, mass illegal migration is not just an economic or humanitarian issue but a deliberate strategy employed by those in power to reshape society in their favour.

As Western societies grapple with the complexities of illegal migration, the political landscape remains volatile. While some politicians benefit in the short term, the long-term consequences of this strategy may lead to deeper societal divisions, increased populism, and a growing rejection of the globalist ideals that have dominated political discourse for decades.

Chapter 6: Who Benefits? Following the Money Trail of Illegal Migration

In the previous chapters, we have explored the myriad complexities surrounding mass migration, from the root causes that propel individuals to leave their homes (Chapter 1) to the geopolitical manoeuvres of states that resist accepting refugees (Chapter 4). We have examined the paradoxical nature of immigration policies in Western nations and how these policies are shaped by political interests (Chapter 5). Building on these discussions, this chapter delves into the financial systems that underpin illegal migration, illuminating a web of beneficiaries that profit from a phenomenon often framed as a crisis.

The Migration "Industry"

The term "migration industry" refers to the vast network of entities and individuals involved in facilitating, managing, and responding to migration. This industry encompasses non-governmental organizations (NGOs), private contractors, humanitarian aid agencies, and governmental bodies. It operates within a framework supported by an intricate mix of public funding and private interests. Understanding who benefits from this migration industry is crucial to grasping the dynamics of illegal migration.

Government Funding and Its Allocation

Governments around the world allocate billions of dollars to manage illegal migration, often justifying these expenditures as necessary for national security, humanitarian aid, or public order. The financial allocation generally flows into several key areas:

1. **Border Security and Enforcement**: Substantial funds are directed toward border patrol agencies, surveillance technology, and military-grade equipment. This funding not only supports the enforcement of immigration laws but also creates a lucrative market for private security contractors who

offer solutions to perceived migration threats.

2. **Detention Centers**: Private companies frequently manage detention facilities where unauthorized migrants are held. The privatization of these services has led to a profit-driven model, with facilities often criticized for substandard conditions and inadequate care. These centres can become overcrowded, and the extended detention periods yield significant profits for their operators.

3. **Humanitarian Aid and NGO Funding**: NGOs play a dual role in the migration landscape. While they often provide essential services such as legal assistance, health care, and housing they also receive significant funding from governments and international agencies. This financial support can create a dependency on continued migration flows to justify their existence and secure ongoing funding. Consequently, some organizations may inadvertently perpetuate the cycle of migration by advocating for the rights and welfare of migrants without addressing the root causes of migration.

4. **Healthcare Services**: As migrants often arrive in vulnerable conditions, there is a burgeoning market for healthcare services tailored to their needs. Hospitals and clinics that cater to this demographic can receive government subsidies, while private health providers may seek to fill gaps in services, capitalizing on the increased demand.

The Role of International Agencies

International organizations, such as the United Nations High Commissioner for Refugees (UNHCR) and the International Organization for Migration (IOM), play crucial roles in the migration ecosystem. They receive significant funding from member states, enabling them to implement programs designed to assist migrants and refugees. However, the funding mechanisms of these organizations can sometimes prioritize the continuation of crises leading to debates about whether their efforts truly alleviate suffering or simply maintain the status quo.

The operational budgets of these agencies often reflect the prevailing political climate; they adapt their strategies based on where funding is available, which can sometimes lead to fragmented responses to migration crises that are not fully aligned with the needs of migrants themselves.

Housing and Infrastructure

As migration patterns shift, certain sectors particularly real estate and housing stand to gain. In many urban centres, landlords and housing providers profit from the demand for accommodations among newly arrived migrants. Governments often allocate funds to subsidize housing for asylum seekers and refugees, inadvertently inflating rental prices in the areas most affected by migration. This can lead to a two-tiered housing market, where low-income residents compete with migrants for increasingly scarce affordable housing.

NGOs, Cartels, and Criminal Enterprises: The Dark Side of Migration Profiteering

While many stakeholders claim to prioritize the well-being of migrants, the reality is often more complicated. Some entities may exploit vulnerable populations for financial gain, leading to a range of abuses, from human trafficking to substandard living conditions. The convergence of profit motives and humanitarian efforts creates a moral quandary that complicates the discourse surrounding migration.

In the complex and often opaque world of illegal migration, many well-intentioned organizations and entities play vital roles in supporting displaced populations. However, interwoven with legitimate humanitarian efforts is an equally powerful shadow economy of non-governmental organizations (NGOs), transnational cartels, and other criminal enterprises that exploit migration crises for enormous financial gain. These organizations, while varying in their methods, are bound by a common goal: profiting from human desperation and vulnerability. This section uncovers how billions in taxpayer money dollars, euros, sterling, and other currencies are siphoned into criminal chains that perpetuate modern-day slavery, as well as the insidious influence these organizations wield to sustain their illegal activities.

The Dual Role of NGOs in the Migration Industry

Non-governmental organizations (NGOs) often occupy a paradoxical position in the landscape of migration. Many NGOs operate with the explicit mission of providing critical services such as legal representation, housing, healthcare, and advocacy to those fleeing persecution, war, and poverty. Yet, within this noble mission lies a darker undercurrent. Some NGOs, knowingly or unknowingly, have become key cogs in the machinery that facilitates and prolongs illegal migration.

1. **Government Funding and NGO Dependency**: NGOs receive billions in taxpayer dollars through government grants and contracts designed to manage the humanitarian aspect of migration crises. This funding is often allocated without strict oversight, allowing certain organizations to inflate their operational budgets while failing to deliver meaningful, long-term solutions. The continuation of migration becomes a vital lifeline for these NGOs, whose existence depends on the persistence of the crises they are meant to mitigate.

2. **Human Smuggling Collaborations**: Alarmingly, reports have emerged of NGOs indirectly collaborating with human smugglers by providing logistical support or legal cover for illegal migrants. Some organizations especially those operating in border regions allegedly coordinate with

smugglers, helping them navigate legal loopholes, evade law enforcement, or secure safe passage for migrants. In return, these NGOs may receive a cut of the profits, blurring the line between humanitarian assistance and criminal complicity.

3. **Aiding Cartels and Criminal Networks**: Certain NGOs serve as unwitting enablers of more nefarious actors, such as cartels and human trafficking rings. By providing "humanitarian corridors" or other forms of support, they may inadvertently funnel migrants into the hands of criminal organizations. Once within these criminal networks, migrants often fall victim to extortion, forced labour, or sexual exploitation modern forms of slavery perpetuated by the same organizations claiming to protect them.

Transnational Cartels: Masters of the Migrant Trade

Criminal cartels and syndicates have long thrived on the exploitation of vulnerable populations, and the migration crisis has become one of the most profitable aspects of their operations. Transnational cartels, particularly in regions like Central America, Africa, and the Middle East, have evolved from drug smuggling and arms trafficking into human trafficking on an industrial scale. Their reach extends from the migrant's country of origin to their destination, where they continue to extort and exploit them long after their journey has ended.

1. **The Business of Human Trafficking**: Migrant smuggling has become a multi-billion-dollar enterprise for criminal cartels. Traffickers charge exorbitant fees to transport individuals across borders, often promising safe passage to Europe, the U.S., or other wealthy nations. However, the reality is far more brutal: migrants are often abandoned in dangerous conditions and left at the mercy of hostile environments or border patrols. For those who survive the journey, many face

continued exploitation, either through forced labour or sex trafficking, upon arrival.

2. **Control of Migrant Routes**: Criminal organizations control the key smuggling routes into Europe, the U.S., and other migrant destinations. These routes often pass through multiple countries, requiring collaboration with corrupt officials, local militias, and smaller criminal groups. Cartels charge tolls at every leg of the journey, turning each stage of the migration process into a revenue-generating opportunity. In some cases, migrants are forced to work off their debts through labour or criminal activity, effectively becoming enslaved by the same networks they paid to escape.

3. **Drug and Arms Trade Linkages**: Human trafficking is not an isolated activity. It is often intertwined with the trade in drugs, weapons, and other illicit goods. Cartels use migrant smuggling operations as a cover for their more traditional activities, further complicating efforts to combat these criminal enterprises. Law enforcement crackdowns on one aspect of cartel activity, such as drug smuggling, often push these organizations to shift focus to human trafficking, as it is equally lucrative and often less risky.

The Role of Corruption and Government Complicity

The vast profits generated by illegal migration create a powerful incentive for corruption at all levels of government. From border guards to high-ranking officials, many public servants are complicit in allowing human trafficking to flourish, often in exchange for bribes or a share of the profits.

1. **Collusion with Border Officials**: In many countries, border security is not merely a question of law enforcement but a profit-making venture. Corrupt officials often turn a blind eye to smuggling operations, allowing migrants to pass

through in exchange for a fee. This collusion undermines international efforts to control illegal migration while enriching both the cartels and the individuals tasked with stopping them.

2. **Misallocation of Public Funds**: Billions in taxpayer money are allocated to humanitarian aid and border security, yet much of it ends up in the pockets of criminal enterprises and corrupt officials. Whether through fraudulent NGO contracts, inflated costs for detention centres, or mismanagement of border security budgets, taxpayer dollars intended to help manage migration crises are instead funnelled into the hands of those profiting from human suffering.

3. **Political Influence and Lobbying**: The migration industry's profits extend beyond the immediate actors involved. Criminal enterprises and complicit NGOs often funnel their ill-gotten gains into political campaigns, lobbying efforts, and media influence. This serves to perpetuate policies that allow illegal migration to flourish. In some cases, NGOs have been accused of actively lobbying for looser immigration laws under the guise of humanitarianism, when, such policies benefit the networks that profit from human smuggling and trafficking.

Modern Slavery: A New Face for an Old Evil

One of the most disturbing consequences of this criminal nexus is the re-emergence of modern slavery. Migrants are often forced into indentured servitude to pay off the debts incurred during their perilous journeys. The debt bondage system, where migrants are coerced into labour until their smuggling fees are "paid off," traps individuals in a cycle of exploitation which not many escape.

1. **Forced Labor and Exploitation**: Migrants, especially

women and children, are highly vulnerable to exploitation in the form of forced labour, domestic servitude, and sex trafficking. Cartels and other criminal organizations use migrants as disposable labour, knowing that many will never report abuses for fear of deportation or retaliation. This exploitation occurs not only in the countries of transit but also in the destination countries where migrants seek refuge.

2. **Sex Trafficking and Gender-Based Violence**: Women and girls are disproportionately affected by the migration crisis. Many fall victim to sex trafficking rings that prey on their vulnerability. In regions where law enforcement is weak or corrupt, entire networks exist solely to traffic women for sexual exploitation. NGOs, ostensibly working to combat trafficking, are often ill-equipped or compromised, allowing these atrocities to continue.

A Corrupted System in Need of Reform

The financial and criminal ecosystems that thrive on illegal migration are far more than opportunistic. They are carefully structured, well-financed, and deeply embedded within the global migration industry. NGOs, while offering crucial services, can be complicit in sustaining illegal migration patterns and aiding criminal networks. Cartels and trafficking syndicates have mastered the art of exploiting migration flows, turning human suffering into one of the world's most profitable illicit trades. Meanwhile, government corruption and mismanagement of taxpayer funds allow these activities to flourish unchecked.

The billions flowing through this system do not simply disappear. They are used to buy political influence, corrupt law enforcement, and sustain an economy of human exploitation. If this dark side of migration is to be addressed, it will require not only cracking down on criminal networks but also evaluating how governments allocate funds and monitor the activities of NGOs. Reform is essential, not just to combat illegal migration, but to end the modern-day slavery it has fueled.

Conclusion: A Complex Interdependence

In summary, the financial underpinnings of illegal migration reveal a complex interdependence among various actors from governments and NGOs to private contractors and health services. While the motives of these stakeholders may differ, the outcome remains a significant financial ecosystem built around the phenomenon of migration. Understanding this intricate web of beneficiaries allows us to critically assess the existing policies and practices, paving the way for more humane and effective solutions that address not only the symptoms of migration but also its root causes, as discussed in Chapter 1.

As we look to the future, it becomes imperative to challenge the narratives that frame migration solely as a burden, recognizing the multifaceted realities of the migration industry and advocating for a balanced approach that prioritizes the dignity and rights of all individuals involved. The next chapter will explore potential pathways toward more sustainable migration policies that not only alleviate the immediate pressures but also confront the systemic issues that drive people to leave their homes.

Chapter 7: Cultural Identity in Flux: The Transformation of Host Nations Under Unwanted Migration

Mass migration is arguably one of the most contentious and politically charged issues of the 21st century. In Western Europe, the United Kingdom, and the United States, immigration has long been a subject of debate. However, what makes the current situation unique and especially troubling for many is the fact that this unprecedented influx of migrants is happening against the will of large portions of the native populations. In many cases, mass migration was neither openly discussed nor voted for by the citizenry. Instead, political elites have implemented these policies, either unilaterally or with minimal transparency, leaving citizens feeling betrayed, powerless, and held captive to decisions they never sanctioned. This chapter will examine the sociocultural consequences of this imposed migration and the profound impact it has had on the host nations.

The Disconnect Between Political Elites and the People

The traditional democratic contract between government and the people has always hinged on the idea of consent policies must be proposed, debated, and ultimately voted on by the electorate. Yet, when it comes to mass migration, this fundamental principle seems to have been bypassed in many Western nations. While issues such as healthcare, education, and taxes are typically front and centre in election campaigns, mass migration a policy with enormous social and cultural ramifications has often been neglected or obscured.

In countries like the UK, the US, and across Western Europe, many citizens express the sentiment that migration was never part of the political agenda they supported. In the UK, for example, successive governments since the early 2000s have overseen large waves of migration, despite many citizens particularly in working-class areas expressing concerns over cultural change, social cohesion, and economic impact. These concerns were largely ignored or downplayed by political elites, who often promoted the benefits of migration without addressing its more complex social consequences.

In the United States, while immigration has long been a part of its identity, the surge in unauthorized immigration, combined with changing immigration policies, has frustrated many. Critics argue that governments have imposed mass migration on the population without adequate border control or respect for public opinion.

This disconnect has left many feeling that their voices are being ignored and that their nations are being transformed in ways they did not approve of. As a result, migration has become not just a policy issue, but a question of democratic legitimacy.

The Sociocultural Impact of Imposed Mass Migration and Erosion of Traditional Values and National Identity

One of the primary concerns voiced by those opposed to mass migration is the perceived erosion of national values and identity. In countries with rich cultural histories, such as Britain and France, the influx of migrants often from countries with vastly different traditions, values, and norms has triggered fears that the core identity of the nation is being eroded without the consent of the people.

In France, for example, the republican ideal of *laïcité* (secularism) is being challenged by the presence of large Muslim communities, whose religious practices often clash with the state's secular values. Public debates over the wearing

of religious symbols, such as the hijab, have led to polarized positions, with many French citizens feeling that their cultural heritage is being undermined by policies that prioritize multicultural accommodation over national cohesion.

In the UK, debates over immigration often highlight concerns that British values such as the rule of law, freedom of speech, and gender equality are being sidelined in favour of appeasing migrant communities who may not share these ideals. The rapid demographic changes, particularly in urban areas, are often viewed as an unchosen social experiment, with local populations feeling increasingly alienated in their own country.

Opponents of mass migration argue that this cultural shift is not a natural evolution but rather an imposition by political elites who have chosen to pursue globalist policies at the expense of national sovereignty and identity. Critics often claim that the wholesale transformation of their societies has been thrust upon them without adequate consultation, leading to a loss of the cultural bonds that once unified the nation.

Multiculturalism Without Consensus: Fragmentation Over Integration

The dominant political narrative in many Western countries promotes multiculturalism as a virtue, often claiming that diversity enriches a nation. However, when multicultural policies are imposed without public consensus, the result is frequently social fragmentation rather than integration.

Citizens in host countries often report feeling as though they are being forced to accept a new societal norm, where their own culture is just one among many competing identities, rather than the dominant framework. In towns and cities across Europe and North America, many native citizens find themselves living in communities that have been fundamentally altered by migration. Neighbourhoods once defined by shared language, customs, and traditions are increasingly divided by cultural enclaves where migrants, rather than integrating, often live in parallel societies. These communities can be insulated from mainstream culture, sometimes adhering to values and practices that conflict with the host nation's laws and customs.

For example, in the UK, there are areas where English is rarely spoken, and traditional British customs are seldom observed. Critics argue that these parallel societies contribute to a loss of social cohesion and exacerbate tensions between migrant and native populations. Rather than fostering unity, they claim, multicultural policies have led to fragmentation, with different cultural groups living side by side but seldom interacting in meaningful ways.

In many Western nations, there is growing resentment among citizens who feel they are being forced to accommodate new cultures without reciprocal efforts from migrants to adapt to the host nation's values. This sense of cultural imposition, rather than mutual adaptation, has led to deep divisions and a growing sense of alienation.

Language Barriers and the Breakdown of Communication

One of the most visible indicators of the challenges of mass migration is language. For centuries, language has served as a unifying factor in nation-building, providing a means through which people communicate, engage in public life, and form a collective identity. However, in many Western countries, the arrival of large migrant populations who do not speak the local language has exacerbated feelings of division.

In countries like the US and the UK, language barriers are contributing to social isolation among migrant communities. Critics argue that political leaders have failed to prioritize language acquisition and instead allowed bilingualism or even the non-use of the national language to proliferate. This not only makes integration more difficult for migrants but also alienates the native population, who feel as though their cultural norms are being disregarded.

For native citizens, walking through neighbourhoods where their language is no longer spoken or even visible on public signs can heighten the sense that they are losing control over their communities. This linguistic shift contributes to the growing feeling that national identity is being diluted another consequence of mass migration that was never voted on or discussed transparently with the electorate.

The Breakdown of Social Cohesion

The imposition of mass migration has not only reshaped cultural identity but also challenged the social fabric of host nations. Social cohesion the idea that a society operates smoothly when its citizens share common values, goals, and a sense of belonging is increasingly under threat in countries experiencing rapid, unwanted demographic change.

The rise of populist movements in Europe, the

UK, and the US is, in part, a reaction to the growing frustration among citizens who feel that their countries are being transformed without their consent. Parties that once existed on the political fringes have surged into the mainstream, largely because they have tapped into the concerns of ordinary citizens who feel unheard by the political class. Movements like Brexit, the rise of right-wing populism in Europe, and the election of Donald Trump in the US are all, to varying degrees, responses to the perception that mass migration is being imposed from above, with little regard for the will of the people.

Social fragmentation, fueled by cultural and economic divisions, has become a breeding ground for political polarization. As communities grow more segregated along ethnic and cultural lines, the prospect of a shared national identity becomes increasingly difficult to achieve. Citizens feel less connected to their nation, and the sense of belonging that once unified them is eroded.

National Identity in Crisis

For many in the host nations, the imposition of mass migration has thrown national identity into crisis. What it means to be British, French, or American is no longer a shared understanding among citizens but rather a contested concept.

The rapid demographic and cultural changes caused by migration changes that were neither debated nor voted on have left many feeling as though their country is being taken from them.

Political elites and globalist advocates may promote the idea of a fluid, globalized identity, but for many ordinary citizens, national identity is rooted in a shared history, language, and set of values. The erosion of these bonds without the consent of the people has led to feelings of displacement and resentment.

Conclusion: Restoring Democratic Accountability

The cultural, social, and political impacts of mass migration on Western nations cannot be overstated. What makes this issue particularly volatile is not just the scale of migration but the fact that it has been imposed on the population without their consent. The growing sense of frustration among citizens is not merely a reaction to the presence of migrants but also the perceived betrayal of their political leaders.

Restoring democratic accountability will be essential in addressing the consequences of mass migration. Political leaders must begin to acknowledge the legitimate concerns of their citizens and engage in transparent debates about the future of national identity. Only by doing so can they hope to rebuild the trust that has been eroded by years of unaccountable governance and imposed demographic transformation.

Chapter 8: Hybrid Warfare: Is Mass Illegal Migration a Strategic Tool?

In the rapidly evolving landscape of modern conflict, warfare has expanded beyond traditional battlefields. Asymmetric and hybrid tactics are increasingly employed by state and non-state actors alike, leveraging unconventional tools to achieve strategic objectives. One of the more controversial and often overlooked instruments in this realm is mass illegal migration. This chapter will investigate the hypothesis that mass migration, particularly when illegal, may serve as a deliberate weapon within the broader framework of hybrid warfare. We will explore whether hostile states or non-state actors exploit migration to destabilize Western societies, either by design or opportunistically.

Building on the foundations laid in earlier chapters particularly Chapter 1's exploration of the root causes of migration and Chapter 5's examination of the political dynamics in Western countries this chapter will analyze the potential for mass migration to be used as a strategic lever by adversarial nations. As we move through these topics, the evidence for such strategies, the mechanisms of implementation, and the broader implications for national security will be assessed.

Defining Hybrid Warfare and Strategic Migration

Hybrid warfare refers to the blend of conventional military force, cyber tactics, disinformation campaigns, economic pressure, and other non-military methods to destabilize an opponent without engaging in open conflict. Migration, traditionally viewed as a social and humanitarian issue, becomes a tool in this context a means of generating strain on economic, political, and social infrastructures.

As seen in **Chapter 1**, various factors like war, economic hardship, and persecution have driven migration for centuries. However, there is increasing concern that adversarial states or terrorist networks could deliberately promote mass migration as part of a strategy to undermine the political cohesion of Western societies. **Chapter 5** has already touched upon the political advantages that mass illegal migration can present to populist movements in the West. Here, we will expand that lens to consider how hostile actors might exploit this phenomenon to erode unity and increase social tensions within targeted nations.

Historical Precedents: Manipulating Migration for Strategic Gain

While the idea of weaponizing migration may seem novel, there are historical precedents. During the Cold War, both the Soviet Union and the United States exploited migration flows for political purposes. One notable example was the deliberate promotion of emigration from East Germany to the West to destabilize the communist regime. The forced displacement of populations during World War II also serves as a grim reminder of how migration can be manipulated to achieve strategic objectives.

In contemporary times, migration crises in Europe such as those stemming from the Syrian civil war have raised concerns about whether such crises are being fueled or exacerbated by external actors. Some analysts argue that Russia, in particular, has sought to exploit migration to divide the European Union and weaken NATO cohesion. By supporting regimes that drive their populations to flee or by facilitating human smuggling networks, such actors can create waves of migrants that overwhelm Western systems.

Migration as an Economic and Political Weapon

Mass migration places significant economic strain on host nations. **Chapter 3** explored the economic burden that third-world emigration often places on public resources, such as healthcare, education, and housing. When a host nation's capacity to absorb migrants is exceeded, the result can be an increase in unemployment, lower wages, and heightened competition for public services fueling resentment among native populations.

From a strategic perspective, adversarial states or non-state actors could exploit these tensions to weaken Western societies. Migrants may be used to accelerate social divisions, inflame populist sentiments, and sow distrust in government institutions. **Chapter 7** delves into how the cultural identity of host nations transforms under the strain of absorbing large migrant populations, leading to further polarization. In this chapter, we will examine whether these transformations are being deliberately provoked by external actors to weaken the fabric of Western societies.

Destabilization through Political Polarization

One of the most insidious effects of mass illegal migration is its potential to increase political polarization. In democracies, this polarization can lead to governance paralysis, as we've seen in **Chapter 5**, where political factions use immigration issues to galvanize their bases. The rise of far-right populist movements in Europe and the United States is often attributed to the perceived failure of governments to address the challenges posed by immigration.

Hostile actors may seek to amplify these internal divisions. Disinformation campaigns targeting migrant communities or stoking fears among the native population can exacerbate existing tensions, as seen in previous chapters discussing the influence of global powers like Russia and China. By promoting narratives that pit migrants against natives, or that frame migration as an existential threat to cultural identity, hostile states could encourage the growth of nationalist movements that, in turn, weaken democratic institutions.

The Role of Terrorist Networks and Non-State Actors

Non-state actors, including terrorist networks, may also play a role in promoting mass migration as part of a broader strategy to destabilize Western countries. Terrorist organizations could infiltrate migrant flows, as suggested by certain Western intelligence agencies, planting operatives within refugee populations. This tactic serves the dual purpose of undermining public trust in migrant communities and threatening national security.

Furthermore, organized crime syndicates and smuggling networks often have symbiotic relationships with terrorist groups. These entities can financially benefit from human trafficking while also promoting instability in target nations. The flow of migrants is thus weaponized, both as a source of income and as a vehicle for spreading insecurity and chaos. As explored in **Chapter 6**, there is a complex financial web underpinning illegal migration, and in some cases, following the money trail leads back to hostile state actors who may benefit from the destabilization of Western societies.

Who Is Behind the Strategic Use of Mass Migration?

Several geopolitical actors stand to gain from the destabilization of Western nations through mass migration. Russia, with its history of hybrid warfare, has been accused of using disinformation to exacerbate Europe's migrant crisis. Iran, another key player, may also seek to flood neighbouring regions with refugees to destabilize its adversaries. Similarly, Turkey's manipulation of migrant flows into Europe, particularly during its tense diplomatic relations with the EU, is another example of how migration has been used as a geopolitical bargaining chip.

Non-state actors such as ISIS and other terrorist organizations are also implicated in weaponizing migration to spread instability, as outlined earlier. By using migration routes to infiltrate target countries, they aim to create both short-term security risks and long-term societal fragmentation.

Conclusion: The Future of Strategic Migration in Hybrid Warfare

As the nature of conflict continues to evolve, the use of non-traditional tools like mass illegal migration will likely become more prevalent in hybrid warfare strategies. Migration, when deliberately manipulated, can serve as a powerful destabilizing force, exacerbating economic, social, and political fault lines in Western societies.

This chapter has sought to outline the various ways in which migration may be weaponized by state and non-state actors, linking back to themes explored in previous chapters. As we move forward, Western nations will need to develop more sophisticated responses to these challenges, recognizing that migration is not just a humanitarian issue, but also a potential tool in the hands of adversaries. The focus should be on balancing security concerns with moral obligations, a dilemma that will define the geopolitics of migration in the decades to come.

Chapter 9: The Promoters: Who is Driving Mass Migration to the West?

In the previous chapters, we explored the diverse aspects of mass migration: from the economic and political impacts to the geopolitical maneuvers influencing migration flows. We examined the reasons neighbouring countries often refuse to take in migrants (Chapter 2), how emigration drains public resources in third-world nations (Chapter 3), and how certain nations, such as China and Russia, maintain closed-border policies (Chapter 4). We followed the money trail of illegal migration (Chapter 6), uncovering who profits financially, and investigated the strategic use of migration as a form of hybrid warfare (Chapter 8). In this chapter, we will shift our focus to the promoters the organizations, political groups, criminal networks, and even foreign adversaries driving mass migration to the West. Who benefits, and how do these forces operate?

1. Non-Governmental Organizations (NGOs) and International Organizations

Among the most visible players in promoting mass migration are NGOs and international organizations that operate globally, often under the guise of humanitarian aid. From large entities like the United Nations Refugee Agency (UNHCR) to smaller activist organizations, these groups play a key role in facilitating and encouraging migration.

1.1 Humanitarianism or Migration Facilitation?

While the stated goal of many NGOs is to provide aid and protection to migrants, their actions sometimes go beyond humanitarian work, effectively promoting and enabling mass migration. Many of these organizations engage in search-and-rescue operations in the Mediterranean, a practice that critics argue acts as a de facto shuttle service for illegal migrants attempting to reach Europe. These activities can inadvertently create a pull factor, where migrants are encouraged to embark on dangerous journeys, knowing they may be rescued and brought to European shores.

Beyond logistical support, many NGOs actively advocate for more open borders and looser immigration controls, framing migration as a human right. However, as explored in **Chapter 6**, the financial incentives behind their operations are hard to ignore. NGOs often rely on funding that scales with the number of migrants they assist, creating an inherent conflict of interest. The continuation of mass migration ensures the flow of donations, grants, and government funding.

2. Human Trafficking Networks: The Shadow Economy

Operating alongside NGOs but in the shadows are human trafficking networks, criminal organizations that profit directly from mass migration. These traffickers facilitate the movement of migrants across borders, often in dangerous conditions, and stand at the intersection of a multibillion-dollar underground economy.

2.1 Profit Motives and Exploitation

Human traffickers are driven by pure financial gain, exploiting the desperation of migrants and the weaknesses in international border controls. As discussed in **Chapter 6**, smuggling migrants is a lucrative business, with traffickers charging anywhere from a few thousand to tens of thousands of dollars for passage. These criminal networks often operate with impunity, leveraging corruption in transit countries and capitalizing on the lack of coordination between national authorities. Their operations are fueled by the chaos and instability in regions such as North Africa, the Middle East, and Latin America.

2.2 Collaboration and Loopholes

Traffickers often exploit legal loopholes to sustain their operations. European laws, for example, prevent the deportation of migrants to countries considered unsafe, which creates an opportunity for traffickers to guide migrants into asylum claims. These criminal networks frequently coach migrants on how to present themselves as refugees, even when they do not meet the legal criteria. This exploitation of humanitarian frameworks allows traffickers to use legal protections to perpetuate their smuggling operations.

3. Political and Ideological Drivers of Migration

In addition to financial and criminal elements, mass migration is often driven by political and ideological agendas. Certain political parties, activist groups, and ideologically driven movements see migration as a tool for achieving social and political change.

3.1 Globalist Ideology and the Borderless World

One significant ideological force promoting mass migration is the globalist movement, which advocates for a "borderless world" where national sovereignty is diminished in favour of global governance. Organizations such as the Open Society Foundations have been vocal in promoting open borders and migrant rights as part of their larger vision of global integration. Proponents of this ideology argue that migration enriches societies by promoting diversity, alleviating global inequality, and redistributing populations.

However, as explored in **Chapter 7**, critics point out that this ideology prioritizes the erasure of borders over national security, cultural stability, and economic sustainability. The rapid influx of migrants can strain welfare systems and destabilize cultural cohesion in host countries, leading to political and social unrest.

3.2 Electoral Gains for Political Parties

In many Western countries, political parties also benefit from promoting mass migration, seeing it to secure electoral advantages. Left-leaning parties have been known to support policies that increase migration, assuming that migrant populations especially those reliant on social welfare will align politically with parties that offer expansive government benefits. This phenomenon has been observed in countries like Germany, Sweden, and the United Kingdom, where migrant communities have become key electoral blocs, often tilting the political balance in favour of parties that favour liberal immigration policies.

4. Adversarial States and Geopolitical Agendas

Beyond the internal forces driving mass migration to the West, there is growing evidence that foreign adversaries and hostile states are actively profiting from and promoting migration as part of their broader geopolitical strategies.

4.1 Using Migration as a Weapon

As discussed in **Chapter 8**, mass migration can serve as a form of hybrid warfare, where countries hostile to the West use migration as a tool to destabilize their adversaries. Turkey, for example, has threatened to open its borders and allow millions of Syrian refugees to flood into Europe unless it receives concessions from the European Union. This tactic allows Turkey to exert significant political leverage over European nations while profiting from the financial aid offered by the EU to manage migration flows.

Similarly, Russia has been accused of promoting mass migration to Europe as a destabilizing force. The use of migration as a geopolitical tool is not new, but in the current era, it has become a calculated part of the strategic playbook for countries looking to weaken the social and political fabric of Western nations. By encouraging or facilitating mass migration, these adversarial states can create internal divisions, strain public services, and fuel populist movements that undermine the political stability of their rivals.

4.2 Financial and Strategic Gains

Certain countries hostile to the West, particularly in the Middle East and North Africa, also derive financial benefits from the migration crisis. In addition to extracting political concessions from Europe, these nations receive substantial aid packages, often running into billions of euros, to manage migration. The funds are ostensibly meant to improve conditions in refugee camps and create local opportunities, but corruption and mismanagement mean that much of this money is diverted into the pockets of local elites and government officials.

Libya, for instance, has been a key transit country for migrants heading to Europe. Militia groups, often backed by the state or powerful political actors, run extensive smuggling networks that profit from both the migrants and the European Union's financial efforts to stem migration. These illicit networks fuel instability, perpetuate conflict, and create a cycle of migration that keeps the money flowing.

5. Conclusion: A Complex Web of Motives

The promotion of mass migration to the West is driven by an intricate network of actors, each motivated by their interests financial, political, ideological, or strategic. NGOs and international organizations, while often well-intentioned, blur the lines between humanitarian aid and facilitating migration. Criminal networks profit from human misery, while political parties and globalist movements see migration as a tool for advancing their agendas. Perhaps most alarmingly, foreign adversaries and hostile states use migration as a form of geopolitical leverage, profiting from the chaos they help create and using migration as a weapon to destabilize Western societies.

As discussed in **Chapter 8**, mass migration is not simply a byproduct of global crises it is often a deliberate and coordinated phenomenon, shaped by forces that stand to benefit from the movement of millions of people. These promoters operate across borders, exploiting legal loopholes, financial incentives, and ideological frameworks to perpetuate mass migration, often to the detriment of both migrants and host countries alike. Understanding the intricate web of motives behind mass migration is essential for addressing the challenges it poses and finding solutions that prioritize stability, security, and long-term sustainability.

Chapter 10: The Financial Burden: Draining Public Resources in Health, Education, and Housing

Mass illegal migration is a global concern, raising debates around economic opportunity, humanitarian duty, and the ability of host nations to absorb large numbers of people. One of the most significant and often ignored aspects of this phenomenon is the financial burden it places on public resources. In countries such as the USA, the UK, Canada, and across Western Europe, illegal migration exerts a substantial strain on essential public services, particularly in health, education, and housing. The costs of providing these services often come at the expense of the native population. This chapter examines how these public services are impacted, breaking down the financial costs that taxpayers are shouldering to support migrant populations.

The Financial Scope of Illegal Migration

The scope of illegal migration varies by region, but its financial impact is far-reaching. In the United States, there are an estimated 11 million undocumented migrants, with the number of illegal migrants in the UK reaching hundreds of thousands. Canada and countries in Western Europe, particularly Germany and France, have also seen significant increases in the number of undocumented migrants and refugees in recent years.

While legal immigration involves controlled processes, illegal migration is often unregulated and unquantified, forcing governments to address migrants' needs without proper systems in place for their integration. These hidden costs are then absorbed by public services, placing an often overwhelming financial burden on taxpayers.

Health Services Under Strain
United States

In the United States, the healthcare system, especially in border states like California, Texas, and Arizona, is burdened by providing care to undocumented migrants. The Emergency Medical Treatment and Labor Act (EMTALA) mandates that hospitals treat all individuals, regardless of immigration status or ability to pay. As a result, hospitals lose billions each year on uncompensated care.

For example, Texas alone reports an estimated USD 2.8 billion (approximately GBP 2.2 billion) in healthcare services provided to undocumented migrants annually. These costs are absorbed by hospitals and passed on to taxpayers, contributing to higher insurance premiums for U.S. citizens.

United Kingdom

In the UK, the National Health Service (NHS) faces significant strain from illegal migrants. While the government seeks to recoup costs from non-resident migrants who are ineligible for free care, the NHS loses around GBP 1.5 billion (approximately USD 1.9 billion) annually from unpaid healthcare services provided to undocumented migrants. This shortfall, coupled with an already overburdened system, results in longer waiting lists, delays in treatments, and increased pressure on the healthcare infrastructure.

Canada

In Canada, healthcare is publicly funded and universally accessible, but the influx of undocumented migrants, particularly in major urban centres like Toronto and Vancouver, has led to similar strains. Emergency services, which must provide care regardless of legal status, see millions of Canadian dollars diverted. In Ontario alone, it is estimated that undocumented migrants account for CAD 700 million (approximately GBP 420 million or USD 520 million) in healthcare costs annually.

Western Europe

In Western Europe, the strain on healthcare systems is particularly evident in countries like Germany, France, and Italy. Germany has absorbed over a million refugees since the Syrian crisis, and the cost of healthcare for these individuals has been immense. In 2022, Germany's healthcare system spent approximately EUR 2.5 billion (approximately GBP 2.2 billion or USD 2.7 billion) on providing medical services to migrants. Similarly, France spends around EUR 1.2 billion (approximately GBP 1 billion or USD 1.3 billion) annually, with Italy and Spain facing similar financial challenges.

These financial costs are directly reflected in increased taxes and healthcare premiums for native citizens, as well as in degraded public services due to stretched resources.

The Education Dilemma

United States

In the United States, public schools are required to provide education to all children, regardless of their immigration status. This creates significant financial pressures on school districts, particularly in states with high concentrations of migrants such as California, New York, and Texas. The average cost to educate a child in a public school is around USD 12,000 per year. With an estimated 3.6 million undocumented children or children of undocumented parents, the annual cost of educating these students is about USD 43 billion (approximately GBP 33.5 billion). These costs are paid through property taxes and state funding, often at the expense of native-born students.

United Kingdom

In the UK, the arrival of undocumented migrant children has also placed a heavy financial burden on schools. It is estimated that educating a child in the UK costs around GBP 6,000 per year. With roughly 100,000 children from undocumented migrant families enrolled in public schools, the annual cost is approximately GBP 600 million (approximately USD 740 million). English as a Second Language (ESL) programs, specialized teaching assistants, and additional resources further strain educational budgets, diverting funds from other critical areas such as teacher salaries and infrastructure improvements.

Canada

In Canada, provinces like Ontario and British Columbia report significant expenditures related to educating migrant children. The average cost to educate a child in Ontario is around CAD 12,500 per year (approximately GBP 7,500 or USD 9,000). With thousands of undocumented children entering the system, the annual cost is estimated to be in the hundreds of millions of dollars. This diverts funds from educational initiatives aimed at supporting native students, resulting in larger class sizes and reduced resources for all students.

Western Europe

In Germany, the cost of integrating refugee children into the public education system is high. It is estimated that Germany spends around EUR 6,500 (approximately GBP 5,600 or USD 7,000) annually per child for education. With hundreds of thousands of migrant children enrolled, the annual cost to the education system exceeds EUR 2 billion (approximately GBP 1.7 billion or USD 2.2 billion). France and Italy face similar costs, with both countries reporting hundreds of millions of euros spent on migrant education each year.

The consequence of these rising costs is a reduction in the quality of education for native students, as funds are diverted to meet the needs of migrant children. This can lead to overcrowded classrooms, fewer extracurricular programs, and reduced resources for students requiring additional academic support.

Housing Shortages and Infrastructure Strain

United States

In the USA, the housing crisis is particularly acute in cities with large migrant populations, such as Los Angeles, New York, and Miami. In Los Angeles, the cost of providing emergency housing for migrants is estimated at USD 1 billion annually (approximately GBP 780 million). This adds to an already strained housing market, driving up rents and exacerbating homelessness among low-income residents.

United Kingdom

In the UK, social housing is under intense pressure. Local councils spend approximately GBP 300 million (approximately USD 370 million) annually on emergency housing for migrants, which includes the cost of temporary accommodations such as hotels and hostels. Meanwhile, native citizens often wait years for affordable housing, creating tensions and resentment. This strain on housing resources not only impacts the availability of affordable housing but also results in rising property prices and rents across the country.

Canada

Canada is also facing a housing crisis in cities like Toronto and Vancouver, where housing costs are among the highest in the world. The annual cost of providing social housing and emergency shelter for migrants in Toronto is estimated to be around CAD 350 million (approximately GBP 210 million or USD 260 million). As with the UK, native Canadians are feeling the effects, with longer waiting lists for affordable housing and higher rents across the board.

Western Europe

Germany spends over EUR 1.5 billion (approximately GBP 1.3 billion or USD 1.6 billion) annually on housing for migrants. In cities like Berlin and Munich, the demand for affordable housing far exceeds supply, leading to overcrowded shelters and increased homelessness. France and Italy report similar costs, with millions of euros spent on temporary accommodations for migrants each year. This further intensifies the housing crisis for native populations, driving up property prices and rents.

Infrastructure Strain

Beyond housing, the overall infrastructure in these regions is under severe strain. Roads, public transportation, water, and waste management systems are all affected by the influx of migrants. In many cases, local governments are forced to allocate emergency funds to build or repair infrastructure. For example, Germany recently allocated an additional EUR 500 million (approximately GBP 430 million or USD 540 million) to expand its public transport system to accommodate the growing population.

Diverting Resources from Other Areas of Need

The financial burden of providing health, education, and housing services to undocumented migrants diverts significant resources from other critical areas. In the USA, the USD 43 billion spent annually on migrant education could instead be used for infrastructure repair, mental health services, or educational reform. Similarly, in the UK, the GBP 1.5 billion spent on uncompensated healthcare for migrants could have funded public health initiatives, housing projects, or school improvements. These diverted funds leave native populations struggling with inadequate public services.

Conclusion

The financial burden of mass illegal migration on public resources is immense. Health systems are overburdened, education systems are strained, and housing shortages are exacerbated, all at the expense of taxpayers. While there are strong humanitarian arguments for assisting migrants in need, the costs of doing so are significant and growing. Without comprehensive reform and better resource allocation, these costs will continue to rise, straining public services and leaving both migrants and native citizens at risk of poorer outcomes.

Chapter 11: Policing and Governance: Are Law Enforcement Agencies Compromised?

The phenomenon of mass illegal migration has not only strained the economic, social, and cultural fabric of host nations, but it has also posed profound challenges to law enforcement agencies tasked with maintaining public order and upholding the rule of law. As this chapter explores, law enforcement's role in managing the consequences of migration has become a deeply politicized issue, one that raises questions about the integrity and efficacy of police forces across the Western world.

In this chapter, we will examine whether law enforcement agencies, particularly in the United States and Western Europe, are effectively addressing the national security challenges posed by illegal migration or if their ability to do so is compromised by political agendas. The discussion will focus on the challenges faced by police in dealing with crime, human trafficking, and social unrest linked to migration. Additionally, it will scrutinize governmental directives both domestic and international particularly those issued by Brussels and the White House, which critics argue prioritize political considerations over the safety and security of native populations, especially in border regions and urban centres that are most heavily affected by mass migration.

A Double-Edged Sword: Law Enforcement at the Nexus of National Security and Politics

The role of law enforcement agencies, particularly in Western democracies, has always been to act as neutral enforcers of the law, irrespective of political or social trends. However, as discussed in **Chapter 1: The Root Causes of Mass Migration**, the scale of modern migration waves has created unprecedented challenges for these agencies. Police forces are often the first responders to the multifaceted consequences of mass migration, which can include spikes in criminal activity, trafficking, and public unrest. Yet, their ability to act in the national interest has increasingly come into question, with many suggesting that law enforcement is being co-opted by political pressures.

In the United States, for example, law enforcement agencies such as Immigration and Customs Enforcement (ICE) are central to the government's capacity to regulate immigration. However, as highlighted in **Chapter 5: The Political Advantage of Mass Illegal Migration**, left-leaning political agendas in Washington have not only reduced ICE's operational capacity but also hampered its enforcement of border laws. The White House's cuts to police budgets, particularly in urban areas that serve as migrant hubs, have left police departments undermanned and ill-equipped to manage the increase in crime and social unrest linked to migration. Sanctuary city policies, which shield undocumented migrants from deportation, further complicate law enforcement's efforts by limiting cooperation between local police and federal agencies like ICE.

A similar trend can be observed across Western Europe, where law enforcement agencies have been pressured to follow directives from the European Union, many of which emanate from unelected bureaucrats in Brussels. As discussed in **Chapter 8: Hybrid Warfare: Is Mass Illegal Migration a Strategic Tool?** The EU's policy of open borders, compounded by its bureaucratic directives, has created an environment in which national police forces are forced to prioritize compliance with EU regulations over protecting the security of their citizens. These directives, often formed in the interests of political harmony within the union, have arguably weakened the very institutions responsible for safeguarding the native population.

Crime and Trafficking: The Burden of Enforcement in an Era of Open Borders

Mass migration has been linked to spikes in various forms of criminal activity, ranging from petty crime to organized human trafficking. As noted in **Chapter 3: Third-World Emigration: A Drain on Public Resources?** The influx of migrants can stretch police resources to the breaking point, particularly in urban centres where crime rates have surged in recent years. In cities like Paris, London, and New York, police forces have found themselves on the frontlines of a new form of urban warfare one in which traditional law enforcement strategies are increasingly ineffective.

Human trafficking, in particular, has become a serious issue for law enforcement in regions heavily impacted by migration. Migrants are often subject to exploitation by traffickers who smuggle them across borders in violation of immigration laws. The involvement of criminal syndicates in human trafficking has added another layer of complexity to the policing of migration. As seen in **Chapter 9: The Promoters: Who is Driving Mass Migration to the West?** The financial networks that support these operations are vast, involving both local and international players. The inability or unwillingness of law enforcement to effectively target and dismantle these networks raises troubling questions about whether the police are truly serving the national interest or if they are being held back by political constraints.

The challenges are even more pronounced in border regions, such as the southern border of the United States and the Mediterranean coast of Europe, where law enforcement agencies are often overwhelmed by the sheer volume of illegal border crossings. Border patrols, already under-resourced, are expected to manage not only the flow of migrants but also the smuggling of drugs and weapons that often accompany illegal migration. However, as previously noted, the political climate in Washington and Brussels has constrained their ability to carry out their mandates effectively. Budget cuts, legal restrictions, and political pressure from advocacy groups have all but ensured that these agencies are fighting an uphill battle.

Social Unrest and the Role of Police in Managing Cultural Conflicts

Mass illegal migration has also led to heightened social tensions in many Western nations. As discussed in **Chapter 7: Cultural Identity in Flux: The Transformation of Host Nations**, the rapid demographic changes brought about by migration have sparked conflicts between native populations and migrant communities. These tensions often erupt into public protests, riots, and other forms of civil unrest, placing police forces in the unenviable position of managing both sides of a deeply polarized issue.

In many cases, police departments find themselves accused of either over-policing or under-policing migrant communities. The result is a lose-lose scenario in which law enforcement is criticized for not doing enough to protect native citizens while also facing accusations of racial profiling and excessive force. This dynamic has been particularly evident in European cities such as Malmö, Sweden, and Marseille, France, where migrant enclaves have become virtual no-go zones for law enforcement. In these areas, crime rates have skyrocketed, and police often lack the resources or political backing to assert control.

Moreover, as outlined in **Chapter 6: Who Benefits? Following the Money Trail of Illegal Migration**, various interest groups have a vested interest in maintaining the status quo, further complicating the efforts of law enforcement to restore order. These groups, ranging from non-governmental organizations (NGOs) to multinational corporations, benefit from the cheap labour provided by undocumented migrants and are therefore reluctant to support increased policing of migrant communities.

Government Directives: Compromising the Safety of Native Populations?

One of the most contentious issues in the debate over law enforcement's role in managing migration is the extent to which government directives have compromised police effectiveness. In the

European Union, Brussels has consistently pushed for policies that promote the free movement of people across borders. While these policies are ostensibly designed to foster economic integration and cultural exchange, they have had the unintended consequence of weakening national borders and law enforcement's ability to regulate migration effectively.

Critics argue that these directives prioritize political unity over the safety of individual nations. As discussed in **Chapter 4: Closed Borders: China, Russia, Iran, and North Korea's Stance on Immigration**, other countries have taken a more hardline approach to border security, refusing to bow to international pressure in favour of protecting their national interests. In contrast, Western governments, particularly those aligned with the European Union, have taken a more laissez-faire approach, often at the expense of their own citizens' safety.

In the United States, similar concerns have been raised about the Biden administration's approach to border security. As mentioned earlier, the federal government has scaled back ICE's ability to enforce immigration laws, a move that critics argue has endangered the lives of American citizens, particularly in states like Texas and Arizona that bear the brunt of illegal migration. Furthermore, the defunding of police departments in major cities has further eroded law enforcement's ability to maintain public order, particularly in areas with high concentrations of migrants.

Conclusion: A Compromised System?

In conclusion, the question of whether law enforcement agencies are compromised in their ability to protect native populations in the face of mass illegal migration is a complex one. On the one hand, police forces across the Western world are facing significant challenges in managing the crime, trafficking, and social unrest associated with migration. On the other hand, governmental directives both domestic and international have arguably hamstrung their ability to effectively address these challenges.

As this chapter has explored, the politicization of law enforcement, coupled with the financial and logistical strain imposed by mass migration, has created a situation in which the police are often unable to act in the national interest. Whether this represents a temporary failure of governance or a more systemic problem remains to be seen, but unless significant reforms are made, law enforcement will continue to struggle with the task of managing the complex realities of modern migration.

This chapter ties into earlier discussions on the root causes of migration, the economic and social burdens it imposes, and the broader geopolitical forces at play, offering a comprehensive examination of how law enforcement's role has been compromised and the implications for the future of Western society.

Chapter 12: Solutions and Responses: What Should the US, Canada, UK, and Europe Do?

As discussed in the preceding chapters, mass illegal migration presents a profound challenge to the Western world. It is driven by a mixture of economic hardship, political instability, and strategic manipulations by hostile actors. Addressing this challenge requires a multi-pronged approach, from border control and asylum reform to dealing with criminal elements and hybrid warfare threats. This chapter will propose policy responses to mitigate the risks, focusing on how to reduce illegal migration's root causes, restore social balance through deportations, tackle the criminal underworld enriched by trafficking networks, and respond to potential security threats from hostile state actors.

1. Reforming Border Control Measures

Effective border control is crucial to any migration management strategy. Western nations must significantly enhance their border security apparatus to prevent illegal entry, strengthen internal enforcement to locate and deport criminals and adopt a proactive stance against hostile state actors exploiting migration channels.

1.1 Technological and Physical Measures

- **Biometric Data Systems**: The integration of biometric tracking systems (facial recognition, iris scanning, fingerprinting) at entry points ensures that individuals who enter legally can be traced and that those who overstay their visas or commit crimes can be swiftly identified. Shared databases among Western nations (such as the EU, US, and UK) would allow for better coordination in tracking individuals who move between borders.
- **AI-Driven Surveillance**: Using artificial intelligence and

predictive analytics to monitor irregular migration patterns can provide early warnings of surges and identify trafficking or smuggling networks. This information can guide the deployment of resources to intercept these illegal operations before they cross borders.

- **Physical Barriers in High-Risk Zones**: Although politically contentious, physical barriers combined with high-tech monitoring in key entry points (e.g., the US-Mexico border or certain Mediterranean access points) are essential to deterring illegal crossings. However, these barriers must be complemented by high-tech surveillance and rapid-response units.

2. Deportation of Criminals: A Necessary Strategy?

Deportation of criminal elements is critical to restoring social balance and curbing the influence of criminal networks that thrive on illegal migration. Western nations must adopt more stringent measures for deporting individuals involved in criminal activity while ensuring due process to avoid human rights violations.

2.1 Expedited Deportations of Criminals

- **Legal Reforms**: Loopholes in asylum laws that allow criminals to evade deportation must be closed. Western countries should pass laws that ensure any non-citizen involved in violent crimes, organized crime, or terrorism is subject to immediate deportation after a fair legal process. This would involve revisiting international agreements and securing bilateral treaties with countries of origin to accept their nationals back, ensuring deportations can happen swiftly.
- **Mass Deportations as a Stabilizing Force**: While mass deportations are a drastic measure, they may be necessary to

restore social order, especially in areas where illegal migrants have become entrenched in criminal activities. Organized criminal networks that deal in human trafficking, drug smuggling, and violence often depend on a core of foreign nationals who exploit lax immigration laws. Disbanding these groups through targeted mass deportations could have a stabilizing effect on local communities. However, these actions must be conducted following international human rights standards, ensuring due process is followed.

2.2 Resources to Break Up Criminal Gangs

- **Targeting Criminal Networks**: Law enforcement agencies across the West need specialized units to deal with migrant-driven criminal enterprises, such as drug cartels and human trafficking rings. Resources must be allocated to investigate, infiltrate, and dismantle these organizations, often deeply embedded in migrant communities. Coordinated intelligence sharing between the US, UK, and EU is critical, as criminal networks frequently operate across borders.
- **Financial Tracking and Seizure**: Criminal gangs often benefit from the proceeds of illegal activities, becoming financially powerful. Law enforcement should focus on disrupting these financial networks by freezing assets, imposing sanctions on organizations involved in human trafficking, and pursuing cross-border investigations to cut off the flow of illicit money. Utilizing AI and big data to track money laundering schemes can provide actionable intelligence to dismantle these criminal networks.

3. Dealing with Terrorism Threats: The Hidden Dangers

One of the more sinister aspects of illegal migration is the possibility that hostile states may exploit migration flows to plant operatives in Western nations. This aligns with the concept of **hybrid warfare**, where mass illegal migration can be used as a tool of destabilization (Chapter 8).

3.1 Hostile State Actors and Hybrid Warfare

- **Infiltration by State Actors**: Nations such as Russia, Iran, and China, which have adversarial relations with the West, could use migration as a way to insert covert operatives or foment social unrest. Intelligence agencies in Western countries have flagged the potential threat of terrorists or intelligence operatives entering through the same migration routes used by legitimate refugees. According to some intelligence reports, there may already be sleeper cells waiting for a triggering event, such as a military conflict (e.g., a potential Chinese invasion of Taiwan), to create havoc in the host country. For example, tensions with Iran over its nuclear program have raised concerns that Iranian-backed terrorist groups could use illegal migration routes to embed operatives in Europe and the US.

3.2 Assessing the Threat

- **Quantifying the Risk**: While precise numbers are difficult to obtain, conservative estimates suggest that a small percentage of illegal migrants could be linked to terrorist organizations or hostile state actors. Intelligence-sharing between Western nations is essential to assess this risk. Some studies estimate that less than 1% of illegal migrants may have ties to organized terror groups, but even this small percentage poses a significant risk, given the potential scale of the damage they could inflict.

3.3 Counterterrorism Measures

- **Enhanced Vetting for Migrants from High-Risk Regions:**

Individuals from countries with known links to terrorism, such as Iran or Russia, should undergo rigorous background checks before being granted entry, including detailed security screenings by intelligence services. This would apply not just at the point of entry but throughout the asylum process.

- **Surveillance of High-Risk Individuals**: Western intelligence agencies should coordinate efforts to monitor individuals deemed to be security threats. Those with links to hostile nations, extremist groups, or criminal organizations should be placed on watch lists and surveilled.

4. Streamlining the Asylum Process

Asylum systems are often bogged down by backlogs of applications, many of which are not based on genuine claims of persecution but rather on economic migration. Chapter 5 highlighted how abuse of the asylum system places undue pressure on host countries. Reforming the asylum system is necessary to filter out fraudulent claims and ensure that genuine refugees are given the protection they need.

4.1 Fast-Tracking Legitimate Claims

- **Specialized Courts for Asylum Hearings**: Creating a streamlined legal process with specialized courts that handle asylum claims exclusively would help reduce the time between application and decision. Genuine asylum seekers would benefit from faster processing, while fraudulent claims could be dismissed quickly.

4.2 Safe Third-Country Agreements

- **Processing Centers in Transit Nations**: Asylum seekers could be processed in safe third countries, reducing the number of individuals reaching the borders of Western nations. Agreements should be made with nations in North Africa, the Middle East, and Latin America to establish processing centres where claims can be evaluated before individuals enter the US, UK, or Europe.

5. Long-Term Solutions: Addressing Root Causes

Without addressing the underlying reasons for illegal migration, any policy response will only serve as a temporary fix. Western nations must focus on alleviating the conditions that push people to migrate illegally, as discussed in Chapter 1.

5.1 Targeted Development Aid

- **Stabilizing Conflict Zones**: Western governments should coordinate efforts to fund infrastructure projects, promote education, and provide job training in countries most prone to outmigration. This includes long-term commitments to development aid in regions such as sub-Saharan Africa and the Middle East.

5.2 Supporting Democratic Governance and Conflict Resolution

- **Conflict Prevention**: Western powers must work together to mediate disputes and promote democratic governance in regions experiencing political turmoil. By stabilizing fragile states, the West can reduce the push factors that drive illegal migration.

6. The Political Will to Act

As outlined in Chapter 5, the greatest obstacle to effective migration policy is often political. Mass migration is a politically charged issue, with populist factions on both sides of the debate.

6.1 Building Consensus Across Political Lines

- **Bipartisan Support for Migration Reform**: To effectively tackle illegal migration, governments must build cross-party support. This will require overcoming the polarization that often dominates migration discussions. Politicians need to communicate the benefits of controlled immigration and the dangers posed by unchecked migration.

6.2 Engaging Public Opinion

- **Transparency and Education**: Governments should focus on educating the public about the realities of illegal migration, including both the security risks and the humanitarian imperatives. This would help build public support for necessary reforms, such as tougher deportation laws and more stringent border controls.

Conclusion

Mass illegal migration presents an array of challenges to the US, UK, and Europe. Addressing these issues requires a multi-faceted approach, from securing borders and reforming asylum processes to deporting criminal elements and dismantling the networks that enrich themselves through illegal migration. Western nations must also remain vigilant against hybrid warfare threats while ensuring that humanitarian values are upheld. The political will to act decisively, combined with international cooperation, will be crucial to managing this crisis. With the right policies, the West can restore control over its borders, safeguard its citizens, and fulfil its humanitarian obligations.

Epilogue

As the complexities of mass migration continue to shape global dynamics, this book has sought to shed light on the multifaceted causes and far-reaching consequences of this phenomenon. From the geopolitical strategies of nations to the cultural transformations of societies, migration is more than just the movement of people it is a force that can redefine borders, challenge governance, and alter the very fabric of nations.

In examining these issues, one truth becomes evident: there are no simple solutions. Addressing mass migration requires not only the strengthening of borders and policies but also a deeper understanding of the root causes driving people from their homelands. Global cooperation, long-term strategies, and a commitment to both humanitarian values and national security must work hand in hand to navigate this challenge.

As the world faces an uncertain future, the choices we make now regarding migration will reverberate for generations. The solutions are within reach, but they require a united effort, guided by wisdom, pragmatism, and foresight. Only then can nations balance the needs of their people with the realities of an interconnected world?

End

Don't miss out!

Visit the website below and you can sign up to receive emails whenever John Shenton publishes a new book. There's no charge and no obligation.

https://books2read.com/r/B-A-RJUO-VXQAF

Connecting independent readers to independent writers.

Did you love *Influx*? Then you should read *The Dragon's Gambit: China's Bid for Global Dominance and the Western Response*[1] by John Shenton!

[2]

In the 21st century, few challenges loom as large on the global stage as the rapid rise of China, and it's bid to assert dominance in every sphere of international influence. The Dragon's Gambit: China's Bid for Global Dominance and the Western Response provides a detailed, multifaceted exploration of this phenomenon, offering readers a critical examination of China's strategic ambitions and the global repercussions. This book does more than recount history—it dissects China's current manoeuvres, scrutinizing the far-reaching consequences and posing urgent questions for the West's response.

---

1. https://books2read.com/u/bzyZ9E

2. https://books2read.com/u/bzyZ9E

About the Author

John Shenton was born in Birmingham, England and grew up in postwar England. He spent several years as a Radio Officer onboard a variety of vessels sailing to the Persian Gulf, the Indian Ocean and South China seas.

With degrees and a background in electronics and computers he has lived and worked within the United Kingdom, Germany, Switzerland and Canada.

While doing so, he established numerous trading relationships in Japan, Korea, the USA, China and other countries.

He has been retired for some time now living in Montréal Canada enjoying golfing, writing, sailing and many other things automotive.

About the Publisher

John Shenton published via Draft2digital

www.ingramcontent.com/pod-product-compliance
Lightning Source LLC
Chambersburg PA
CBHW051132160726
47997CB00019B/2317